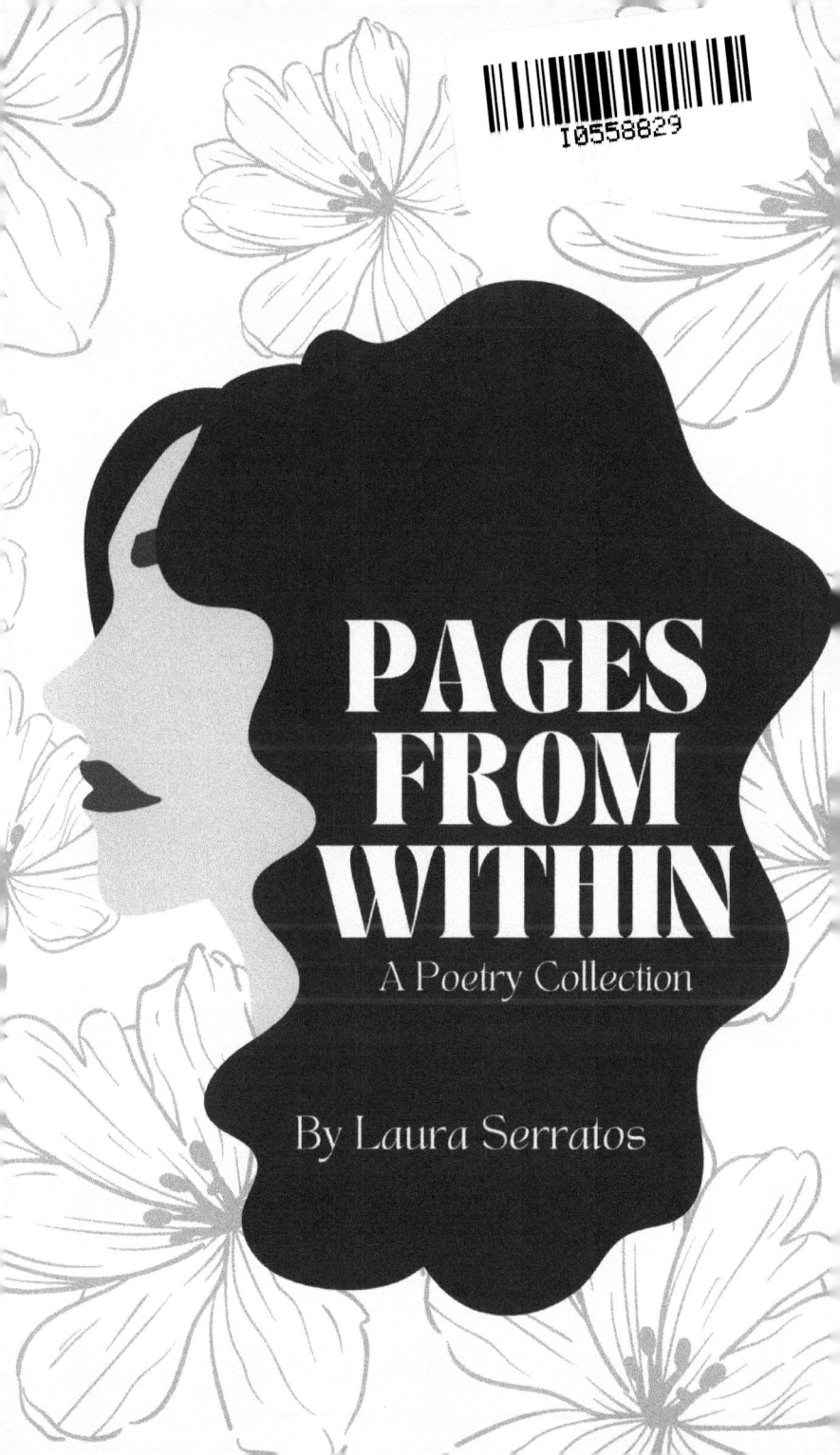

PAGES FROM WITHIN

A Poetry Collection

By Laura Serratos

Laura Serratos

Pages From Within
A Poetry Collection

by

Laura Serratos

ALE*g*RÍA

PUBLISHING

Library of Congress Control Number: 2024901622
ISBN: 9798988174653

Published by Alegria Publishing

Acknowledgements

I want to thank the following people who have over the last year contributed in some way to making this book a reality:

To my husband, Sergio, my son, Christopher, my daughters, Carissa, Christa, and Caralyna, Cathy and my grandson Jude for your understanding and continuous support.

To my mother, Gloria, for always being proud of all the accomplishments her family achieves, big or small.

To my grandparents, father, brothers, sisters-in-law, aunts, uncles, cousins, nieces and nephews, you have all shaped who I am in some way.

To my mentor, Davina Ferreira, whose encouragement, faith, and loving feedback has encouraged me to continue to grow as an artist. You are a true inspiration.

To my Alegría family, who will always be a part of my heart and soul.
We are forever bonded by a love of writing and poetry.

To my dear friends and colleagues, Laura and Kayla, there are no words for what you have done for me on this journey of writing and healing.

Finally, to the reader, for it is you who gives life to my thoughts and words.

Foreword

In late July, I began my new job at the adult high school I would call my home for 3 years. I hadn't the slightest idea what intense hardships awaited me, but they were made much softer and more bearable by the presence in room 102. I don't know what it was about her that called to my soul so deeply, the pull like a magic fairy whose voice trails on the winds in the woods, beckoning the young girl to enter the mysterious forest to find the magic that lies within. In that room, I met Mrs. Laura Serratos, my dear friend and mentor. We were both writers, teachers, and laughers about life's silly moments. There truly was magic for me behind that door.

Studies suggest that when people share suffering, they are brought closer together. I believe this is a truism for Laura and me. The days at this high school were dark for teachers, rife with disrespect and contempt present at every corner. The feelings we shared were like the bitterness of black coffee-the stale kind with grounds embedding the bottom of the cup. The only way I survived was through Laura's hope and her yearning for something greater, as well as her compassion. Listening to her speak of her dreams and wishes was inspiring. Having her hold my hand as I cried, head on her heart, created a safe space where I felt nothing could hurt me. All of this provided the cream I needed for my black cup of coffee, the white, milky tendrils swirling in the cup, giving color back to my life.

Though it seems that in our last year working together, Laura's coffee turned blacker and blacker. I could see the sadness that so oppressed her in room 102. She was only alive when talking about her writing and traveling the world. She was a Calla lily, uncomfortable in the soil she was planted in, ready to grow taller and brighter in new dirt. Her lifeblood and creativity were suffocated in that small green room, the color she so hated and repeatedly told me she wanted to change.

In *Pages from Within*, we see these moments of wilting for Laura, calling to her muse to sustain her. As stanzas go by, we finally see the flower from Laura's previous book, I, Too, Bloom open her petals fully, reaching through the mud to find the sun. She listens to the call of her feminine energy, releases her power, and breathes again.

In reading these pages, I have felt power emanating from within myself. I have never known the power of feminine energy in its full capacity until Laura wrote about what many women feel. We are caged into these roles of mother, daughter, teacher, etc. We are exhausted and at times it can feel that we're being choked to death by the responsibility we have to others. Laura provides hope to the woman who's feeling trapped and hasn't bloomed yet. She shows raw pain as part of the process in becoming a beautiful bloom. Through her poetry, I now remember to listen to the call for my creative passions and understand that hardship is the dirt in which we grow into something beautiful.

Kayla Klein

Preface

"The outpouring of my soul, captured by pen and paper, makes me feel alive."

Growing up, I never thought I could be anything even closely resembling a real writer although I was always encouraged to be creative. My grandfather who was an artist, my grandmother who crocheted, and my father who played guitar expressed their creativity as a fun pastime. So, I began to write. As an eight-year-old, my first short story had no plot and all flat characters, but it was my first attempt at bringing my passion into existence. My journey as a writer began at that moment, and for the last forty-five years, I have been exploring it on and off. Along the way, I felt shy, preoccupied, and fearful of pursuing my passion with any seriousness. Writing this book has helped me change that.

These are the personal snapshots that I have found throughout my search for who I am, where I come from, and who I am still becoming. It has never been easy for me to be completely open. I thought I would offend people if I revealed my feelings. I would often hear, "Children should be seen and not heard." This conveyed to me that I needed to be silent. Composing poetry has helped me become less afraid of being vulnerable and speaking about those things that sometimes feel uncomfortable. I have the chance now to tap into that vulnerability and take a good look at myself in this new season of my life.

After five decades, I realized that any age is the perfect age to start anew. Being a published author later in life gives me the opportunity to see things with wisdom and a mature understanding. As an older woman in my prime, I am at a point where I am choosing to reinvent my career and thus my life in the process. This book encompasses those thoughts that I live out every day in my work as an educator and in my personal life. I will never stop growing and evolving.

Accepting myself as a true author has helped me regain the focus and mindset to push myself in the right direction and take control. I now have the heart to continue my journey as a writer and poet.

Compiling these new pages has helped me to further explore my path as a genuine creator. This poetry collection reflects the deeper feelings and emotions of myself through free verse. Specifically, the themes and subject matter can relate to women who would like to be empowered to begin a creative journey of their own. Widely, it is meant to inspire people of all ages who might need to be encouraged to start working towards their goals and to do what brings them joy and happiness.

I have found love and acceptance in the everyday dealings of life as well as through my childhood memories and the nurturing of my inner artist. I have explored the depths of self-love and realized my true sentiments. The deepest parts of my creativity continue to flourish, and I can confidently communicate the authentic voice that longs to be heard.

Pages From Within continues where my acceptance began with my first poetry collection, *I, Too, Bloom*, to where I am today. I hope as you read these pages you are moved to live your life creatively and do something that makes you feel alive.

To Fully Bloom

What does it mean to fully bloom?
How does it feel to open up your petals?
Does the soft smooth skin relax?
Can you at last inhale?
The world can now see you
You don't want to hide anyway
Being closed up served no purpose
except to protect from the sting of your own
negative thoughts
Opening up can feel unreal at times
like this is not your transformation.
There is pure love waiting, but not what was expected.
You think you need to be pretty to gather admirers.
That can never keep you alive.
A flower doesn't flourish if water soaks it from above.
You need your roots nurtured and fertilized
with love and patience
　　　You are the petal visible to all
　　　You are the strength of the roots
　　　You dig into the earth and ground yourself in the
work no one sees
The beauty they might see doesn't last
Water on a petal can help it glisten, but does it nurture to
the core?
　　　You are stretching beyond your limits
　　　You are facing the sun for one more day
　　　Your fullness, a silhouette in the moonlight
　　　vulnerable but strong
Your skin feels new, not like something to crawl out of
You can breathe at last and know another cleansing breath
is waiting
You exhale confidence while remaining humble

To fully bloom means to hide no more
.

Beauty of a Stranger

She needs no name,
this woman next to me
        On the bus
        In a cafe
        On a plane

Oh, the beauty
        of being open with a stranger

Her eyes tell of wisdom
Her smile sends warmth to my soul
I trust her with my heart
even though she's a stranger

There is something alluring,
crowding my space
or am I in hers?
It doesn't matter
We were meant to share fears
laugh at the world

Faith and belief fill the palms of her hands
I sleep soundly in her energy
Her guidance and comfort soothe me

Just a chance meeting, but
she was my savior
My friend for a whisper of time
Her name alludes my memories
Her kindness impressed upon my heart
I can't imagine a more perfect confidant

Oh, the beauty
        of being open with a stranger

Reign of Power

A goddess is rising like a flame doused with desire
Love only her heart can fuel
A goddess rising from the ash of weak flesh
burned away by self-love
No longer captive inside the broken case
of glass dreams
She can pierce through thoughts
meant to render her powerless
Nothing can stop her reign now
     not a look of judgment
     not a comment behind her back
     not an unkept promise
Her power is limitless in her own reality
where false beliefs dare not intrude upon
her golden peace and calmness
Her stature may say little lady
But her stance says raging woman
Her soul unleashed by wisdom
Time now at her command
She sits on that mountain of courage
ready to come down and smash
every last criticism, doubtfulness, and offense
No need to bow
She's already above the bullshit.

Weight of My Worry

Eyes burning for sleep
Evading my mind, a yawn
stretches over my mouth to catch
air that might relax my fears
It's been a while since I've put words
to my thoughts
But the blurred vision I have
won't let me rest until my hand
has moved across the page
Somewhere between a stiff neck
and shoulders in knots
Lays the weight of my worry
        about losing sleep and sanity
Rolling my neck feels good for the moment
among the crackles and pops of muscle
The loosening of stress are stones of burdens
not mine but somehow in my hands
Only a soothing voice could undo all the pain
and powerful words would give me the rest I seek

My Hand Aches

This phantom ache in my hand
tells me there is a story
waiting to be released by
black liquid love

When I think about certain things
my hand aches
signaling that it's time to write.
There is a story within my soul
longing to fill a page with love.
This ache in my hand doesn't
go away with a flick of my wrist
or a stretch of my fingers
It never leaves, only soothed

Then, the real pain of
Stiffness and numbness radiate
as my hand tells a poem
or quotes my heart
This pain worsens with every quick stroke
and pressure inflicted
by holding my pen
creating a life of thoughts.

My hand never stops aching
to tell what's inside
It must write to soothe
It must write to feel
If I stop… it numbs
If I go…it aches

Don't Ask

If you ask me how I feel,
      I might tell you a lie
            --You only want to hear what's good
If you ask me what I want in life,
      I might tell you a fairy tale
            --You love a happy ending
If you ask me what I think,
      I might try to read your mind
            --And give you back your own thoughts
If you ask me about my dreams,
      I'll tell you about a broken past
            --Nothing matters against your ideal anyway
If you ask me about my day,
      I'll shrug my shoulders indifferently
            --You have never asked me that before, don't
start now
If you ask for my opinion,
      I'll water it down to make it easy
            --You can't take it if it doesn't match yours
If you ask me what I did all day,
      I'll probably get defensive
            --I know you don't honor my self-care
If you ask me what I write about,
      I'll tell you it's really nothing
            –you are only half-interested in my truth
If you ask me what is true,
      I will smile and look away
       –Only I can handle the words that
            Seep from my mind and spill that truth

Where Power Lies

The power we have united
       is greater than working alone
When we breathe together
       sit quietly amongst each other
       listen as the stillness grounds us
       we change the story of us
We create love and comfort
       for those who need it most

We combine our strength to help
       our loved ones overcome obstacles
We offer support, not pity
We walk together on this journey
There is no timeline here
We are present, it is our gift

We don't judge, we listen
Our power is magnified by
       the amount of souls searching for a dream
Living in the past is gone
Worrying about the future isn't needed
We work now for the now
       –where the power lies

We break the bonds of insecurities
We laugh in the face of struggles
We push aside the chains of self-doubt
We change the reality
We challenge the norm

We manifest love and happiness
       where our power lies

I Wish You Knew

I don't think you understand
      the significance of the moment
Your blank stare tells me my words
      mean nothing collectively

Do you think this is unreal?
Your beliefs are limited
      to 9-5 income driven status
It's too far from reality to see
      how close you are to a miracle
A miracle to you, but to me
      my life's droplets of tears
      which pour as one body from my mind
I see the reality while you see
      wishful thinking and backup plans

This is it...there is nothing left
      to hope for, it is here and now
You will see it at once, or you
      won't believe it can be done
But my perspective comprehends
      the grandeur of the things that
      Seem small and unimportant
         –my time and effort without compensation
I'm just at the point of pulling
      myself above the line where your
      eyes naturally go
That's the hidden magic
      of the significant moment
      I wish you knew.

Limited Access

These vibrations in my body
My Energy flowing, waking up
The cool feelings tingle across my skin
You are the protector of my beautiful Energy
        swirling, waiting to release

My Energy lives within my body
I am numb with every breath
        that channels through and around you

I want to keep you safe
I want to guard you
        in the embodied warmth

No one can have access to this
        divine shimmering glow
Never will anyone again take
        what belongs to me
They can only receive
        if they are even worthy enough

This is my purity
This is my divine power
This is my sensual femininity

The precious glow
        of my divine Energy

Love with Peace

I love who I am becoming

Because I love others,
I am on the right path
manifesting
      with every breath

I am kind
I am caring
I am loving

I will continue to evolve

Even if I can't see it,
      everything is working for me
I am letting things be
I am letting people
      who no longer serve me
          Go with peace

My Morning
5am contemplations
When the sky is dark
and the world soundly asleep

My Thoughts Are Alive

I'm keeping my thoughts alive
     giving them life with paper and ink
A reader's eyes animate my thoughts
Creating
     Movement
          Value
            Joy
My writing is an entity
     energized by the universe

Inside of anyone who absorbs my words

Just Free

I want to live my life
        the way I've always imagined

Free to make decisions
        Without guilt
Free to find who I am
        Without paying a price
Free to love the soul who cries out to me
        Without judgment
Free to move my body to the sound of my heart beat
        Without ridicule
Free to explore the world
        Without worry of being a woman
Free to cry
        Without questions
Free to fantasize
        Without shame of my imagination

Just free

Ode to Joy

I felt you in my body once
You've been under my skin
No way to explain how I feel except
my heart wells up to the point
I can barely breathe
When you are with me
a rush of energy flows through my veins.
You never stay for long
You must be giving someone else a thrill
I pick up old books that remind me of you
Do I toss away those brown shoes
that you once walked in?
My favorite pair of earrings are useless
because one you took with you
while the other collects dust
I write to you hoping you understand that
I long for your presence
You are what helps me decide
        On a song,
what movie will play on repeat in my head
How chocolate anything caresses my tongue
You are the treasure I search for
Among memories and shadows

Don't Think

Don't think–
you can glide your fingers over my skin
        and touch my heart
if you squeeze my hips you can arouse
        a flame in my soul
you can rub my thighs
        and enter my feminine depths

Don't think –
because I've shared my body
        That you somehow possess it now
because you've held my hand
        That you have manipulated my mind
because you provide me comfort
        That I won't choose to live in poverty
 because you've invested many years
        That I am not more than a jewel you can cash out

You see–
I am a woman, alive
Made not from your manhood
but by the hand of God
to live
My life
According to my own senses
These things do not rely on you
But I accept and ask you to join me
in my life of splendor and joy

Cool Summer Nights

Late summer nights are for writing out your heart
You'll never get to feel what's inside if you don't come out
The cool night breeze might send a chill up your spine
Don't think about those images that stay burned in your mind
You need to shift so you live a life of peace
What might happen is of no concern to you now
Keep the flame in your place of desire burning
The ache in your hands tell of a poem yet to spin
Old wounds open and set you back for a minute
You're not meant for times of lust; your body is precious
Don't let the red flags sway in front of your eyes without
Knowing you have the power to turn them
To pink ribbons with shear thoughts on a cool summer night

No Limits

Don't tell me I have limits when I've pushed through
my own screwed up beliefs meant to keep me bound by fear

Don't try to put a cap on the amount of success
that you think is achievable for me

I have listened and learned long enough to know
I have yet to reach heights of unknown potential

Don't tell me my thinking doesn't make sense because you can't
reason with a notion created outside of your paradigm

My perspective has changed to a vision of creative
proportions, which your eyes cannot perceive

I know what is meant for me regardless of what your senses
tell you
Mine tell me I'm beyond the walls of small imaginations and
weaknesses

My Best Competitor

Comparing myself to others used to be a daily activity,
which left my soul exhausted

Believing I couldn't measure up to the standards set too high
by my own fear of rejection

Competing against a contender who existed in a greater light
than my dim inward view of myself

Struggling to keep a spot in a place
where I was not welcome anyway

Reaching out to myself was pointless
since I was the one pulling away

Feeling invisible tore my spirits to shreds
Hoping someone would see my effort

Looking in all directions for acceptance
only made my head and heart dizzy

Wondering if I would ever please people
who could make me feel like an equal

Accepting that no one else was in this contest except myself
and my best competitor was me

Knowing that each day I look in the mirror at the one
who is my competition and support

Reflecting on all the negative talk in my head
gives me the determination to start a new contest

encouraging the woman in the mirror to keep moving forward

Most Days

There are days when the air is good enough
to fill my lungs with peace and calm
Closing my eyes brings joy
to my heart and head
There are days when a single breath is all I need to feel
my body changing spaces and drifting off to dreamy
places
There are days I float away on a cloud
of possibilities that bring me to a state
of contentment and slow harmony
There are days when my body and mind cannot fathom
a moment of calm because some thoughts are stronger
than my breathing rhythms
There are days I know I've learned to change
and shift out of old patterns of confusion
But most days
I am sure that my spirit is soaring across a sky of starlike
dreams
meant for me to reach

Password to Peace

To all the negativity
that persits to enter my life
in ways disguised as reasonable

To the images of my past self
which slide across my mind and bring
self-loathing with it

To the old ways of spiraling
out of control with regrets of decisions
made at vulnerable times

To digging up all the
old feelings of self-conscious
thoughts wrapped in fear

To putting myself last
so others can be first although
it was not soothing to my soul

To shrinking to the size of a seed
that allowed others to grow and bloom
while I was stuck in rocks and sand

I say-
"Hell no"
        (the password to my inner peace)

Drop of Love

The tear running down my check
is an endless drop of love.
It may appear to be single,
but it carries a lifetime of emotions.
There is a well in my chest
that is overrunning with the love
of a mother's soul.
One tear can equal a sea
of heartfelt cries
and collected sentimentalities.

Palm Tree Dreams

Palm tree leaves in a warm tropical breeze
rustle and sway through coconut scents
and a blue sky dabbed with white clouds
Yellow
Green
Brown
Tanned by the Caribbean sun
Black birds perch on your sacred branches
as they call to each other
and summons my tropical mood

You never bend to the thoughts
and dreams of anyone
who sees you
as anything other than
a symbol of quiet calm

Mexico

The smell of seaweed is etched in my memory
The cool breeze caresses my hair and skin
Blue and white waves roll and tumble
From depths beyond my eye
A place I've never known, but my senses will never forget.

Welcome Home

I enter the port for the car
to take me on its hour drive
to the place I've waited to see
I don't quite fit in here
I don't have a native's tongue,
The man who greets me
chuckles at my lack of culture
 yet he understands who I am
and says, "Welcome home"
At that moment, I knew that someday
I would return.

Moon Over Mexico

You look different
from where I now stand
I've seen you before
among rooftops and towers
Here, palm trees
gently brush your face
with the ocean breeze
High above the clouds
you are a precious pearl
I want to hold
in the palm of my hand
Your energy fuels my spirit
I may never again see you
from this point of view
but your glow illuminates
my memories of Mexico

What I Feel

Sometimes words are not enough
to convey what I feel inside
My chest wells up
and I cannot contain my energy
I feel it bubble and rush
through my veins
But even these words
that I have given you
are not adequate
You must feel what I feel
to know what I know
when every part of my body
feels overcome with hope

I Am Grounded

I stepped outside
looked up to the sky
meditated with my face
in the light blue breeze
I was moved
to slip off my shoes
I needed to feel the earth
with bare feet
The sun's warmth
massaged my head
I was connected to earth and sun

I affirmed that space
It was only for me
I was one with the universe

I am timeless
I am limitless
I am grounded

Morning Magic

Every morning I drink a magic potion
 it holds positive ideas, thoughts, and words

living energy flowing through my body
quenches me after a night of deprivation

Slowly and intentionally
I sip this refresher
It seeps into every cell in my body
it absorbs into
my muscles
my organs
my mind

It flows into my well being,
moisturizes my lips,
cools my tongue

My magic morning drink

A Beautiful September Morning

A deep sadness hung over me
I know you felt it too
Already deep in grief
from a year of loss and pain
The world seemed so scary and cold
Time stopped for a short while
My thirty one years a mere droplet
among waves of tears
I had to question life
nature
myself
for waiting so long
It took a day of death
to bring focus on life

Twenty years vanished like mist
We became strong
I became stronger
I needed to feel alive
My mind molded around
writing and words

I never forgot you
I forgot me
On this day, I honor you
by remembering that my life is a gift
wrapped in scenes and sounds
of a beautiful September morning

Love

I don't know what I'm supposed to write for you.
I refuse to get caught up in words of sadness and fear.
I'm not afraid to say something good has come from a bad place.
Should I thank you for showing me what I needed to change?
Will my words somehow make things better when you think about
all that has been done?
I don't know the words I'm supposed to find
to give you a sense of peace.
I'll never understand the need to push people away to create a better life.
Being alone isn't the answer, especially when words need to be heard from your lips.
I'm aware I was never going to be the one to bring you happiness and joy,
but that doesn't mean I haven't found a piece of it for myself.
Why do we hurt the ones who love us the most?
It's just a question.
I don't need an answer.
I don't need anything except my pen and paper to write words,
words you think you want to read.
 I won't let you read anything that sounds sad or hurtful.
All you need for me to write for you is one word
The one you need impressed upon your mind
Too hard to say with your lips
Too foolish to feel with your heart
You want me to write something for you?
Here it is…
              Love!

I Give It Power

I am in a world that obsesses and validates youth and
beauty
I admit, I desire some of that validation
but I know true beauty
comes from inside

I have it deeply rooted in me
where it is grown and nurtured
Ready to manifest into the world

People see the fruit of a healthy seed
filled with love, beauty, confidence
 self-worth and value

I have the ability to nurture it
to give what it needs to grow and bloom,
Like a blossom finally come to life

I make it grow
I give it life
I give it power

Its beauty and strength depends on me
I am the product of my inner world

Lunar Energy

White moonbeams on water
Crystals purified by lunar energy
The fullness of tonight
Stirs my heart and soul

Morning Mirror

I arise before the sun
and catch a glimpse in the mirror
Golden brown waves
down my shoulders and back
A hint of silver streaks
show wisdom of days and nights
spent contemplating who I am

My face
reflecting a private life
My eyes
looking through my soul
Lines of laughter
showing decades of happy memories

But I love what I see
My perfect imperfections
staring back at me
With a smile and a wink
I am ready for the day

Coming Out of The Shadows

I was afraid of the dark for a long time
I was told there must be something within me
that made me fear the absence of light

I have witnessed many others walk into dark rooms
eager to help me find the light switch
I envied their bravery, but it was not enough
My admiration could not outweigh my fear

I was told I would outgrow it
Someday I would be brave enough
to enter that room without my heart racing
or being terrified of something to destroy me

They were right
It was a phase
I am coming out of the shadows

Where I Belong

Where I belong
is between here and there
That simple space
between sleep and awake
I feel the realness
of a place with no existence
Sometimes I want to stay
in that confusion,
not knowing what is imaginary

Sometimes I can't believe
what my eyes say is real
I'd rather be at the doorway of drowsiness
which is where I find acceptance
Where I belong

The Power of Voice

My word choice and arrangement
        create the feelings
        I wish to give to you
My attitude toward the subject
        offers affection or indifference
My point of view
        dictates the story being told

This is how you will know me
This is how I know myself

I give hope a voice
Disbelief is silenced

Time of Wonder

The small stretch of time
when the end of night
dissolves into the start of day
is a time of wonder for me

I see
Beauty peaking
Flaws barely visible
A perfect shade of blue
Snow on the ground
Lights reflecting
The day opening up

Keep me in dawn
Where I am fully present

This Morning

Morning comes alive
when lights turn on
I crave a caffeinated sip
to get me through the day

Emptying out my thoughts
Is a ritual not taken lightly

Headlights beam across the window
Silhouettes move in the background
The precious quiet
helps me focus my intentions

This morning is like many others
yet unique
Tomorrow will be different too

Floors creaking from feet above me
Tell me it's time

This morning is alive

Dream Big

Broadway actress, singer, dancer
Star on a New York stage
Lights shine down on a dream
as roses sprinkle at my feet

Rome, Paris, London bridge
Travel first class day and night
They love to say my name
It rolls off tongues of kings and queens

Author, writer, poet
A best-selling attitude
A poetry book to immortalize
my creative gift to the world

Silver screen queen
Hollywood calling me
Overnight television sensation
Limousine rides to the studio
Red carpet evenings

Dinner in Spain
Coffee in Paris
The world now in my hands
like a crystal menagerie

Don't tell me not to *dream big*
You'll see my name written across time
And roaring with the wind

Not Just a Fantasy

My childhood fantasy
was to be a superhero
Wonder woman
Bat girl
Catwoman
      yes, a villain
      but she wore it well

Magic lassos
Crystal clear airplanes
Motorcycle rides
A secret hiding place

I imagined I had power
It felt real in my world

I realize
There *is* real power in me
Not just a fantasy

I am a woman of wonder
I am a secret world
I can live many lives

No longer just a fantasy

Finding Happiness

Finding happiness is as easy as
making a cup of tea
All of my senses activated
Soaking up the sweet steam
My soul's act of love
for the one who needs joy
Happiness for me

Feeling Lost

I get lost in the sound
of my hand sliding across paper.
My pen clicking with each stroke
leaving marks
to help me find the way.
Even when I'm happy,
I love feeling lost in the sounds
of my own creativity.

True Happiness

Find happiness within yourself
Don't look to others
Only you know what it takes
      to bring heaven into your life
Consider your own mood
One moment you feel joy
      in the blink of an eye
      you might feel disappointment
Don't rely on the ever changing
      feelings or emotions of another person
You will only get what they feel at the moment
Seek what truly brings you pleasure
Keep it close
You will know when you need it
      and you will never be disappointed
The only person
who can bring you
True happiness
is you

Deep Breath

I breathe deeply
taking in life
I exhale slowly
releasing the tightness
in my chest
A steady cycle of breath
creates a coolness
through my veins
Vibrations of energy
surge through my body
I am unbound by time
Numb with bliss
Weightless
in body and mind
I'm different
just by a sliver
I return
free

Letting Go

I need to let go-
> Of the things not meant for me
> The ideas that keep me limited
> Daydreaming of the past
> Making others feel comfortable
> Wishing things were different
> Hoping someone else will change

I need to move on without guilt

I need hold on to
> My assumptions
> My dreams
> My desires

I am stretching my hands in the air
and taking hold of myself

Connected

Bare feet in the ground
Face towards the sun
I bloom
    in the glory
    of rays warming my body
    soaking up the energy
    in a meditative sway
    as sounds of nature
    recharge my mind

I am surrendered
to the earth and sun

Guilt

It keeps me where
I don't want to be
It tears me from
my dreams and desires
It is deeply rooted
within me
Unsure of where the seed
was planted
but it flourishes
like a weed
It tries to kill the beauty
Of daydreaming
Once it's gone
I can go where
I want to be

Arrive On Time

When you find that certain time
When your creativity flows like a river
Make it a point to arrive on time
Don't let anything stop you
from engaging with your muse
She will always be there
waiting to wrap around your spirit
Sure, there are other times of the day
There is that one moment
where you capture the best
of who you are creatively
It is the most pleasing
the most satisfying
to your soul

Before Dawn

Before dawn
I write
As it breaks,
light shines
to show the world
my imagination
The peak
of my creativity
transitions
with the night
A precious few
minutes
where I disappear
into a world
of hope
and words

Day By Day

It's hard to see change
when you look
day by day
Same old routine it seems
Work all day
Dream all night
Waiting for a sign
that everything is alright
Stuck in a spiral of
      should have been
      could have been
But when you remember
who you are
it's easy to see changes

Keep moving forward
Even the smallest step
puts you ahead
and straightens out
the twisted words in your head

Let Truth Guide

I did myself a favor
I set my mind free
I spoke up
through shaky hands
A restless night followed
A morning headache too
but I'm free because
what was caged
inside my heart
has been released

There's no going back
Just moving forward
I'll let truth guide
My next step

Meant For More

Meant for more than dreaming away the day
down the same old route over the bridge
Hypnotized by this familiar drive
and bumps in the road
No creativity with hands
on the steering wheel
No connection to nature
When feet are on metal
Twenty-five minutes there and back
Wasted mediation time
Surrounded by ideas but
unable to accelerate to catch up
on dreams for the day
Meant for more than a misdirected
creative life

Mane

My hands caress you
Tangled between my fingers
I gently undo your knots
Your slick strands flow
Passed me and I inhale
a sweet botanical breeze
You bend at my every whim
As long as I brush
and massage you at the core
I love you, Mane
My Brown
Gorgeous
Pride

A Poet's Dream

A cup of green ginger tea
Honey swirls around the cup
Sweet scents relax the mood
Words drift in and out
like a half-forgotten dream
Scraping the land of wishful thinking
as jazz plays to my soul

Creating stories untold
Sharing feelings never released
Shifting from woman to poet

The reality of my hand
The paper canvas sealed
by my inner being
Sometimes easily flows
Others stuck in time
but always living
in a poet's dream

What I Need

What are the words I need to hear?
What can I tell myself?
What words can I say
to make things right?
I never knew that I should only count on me
I mean, I did but I thought
I was wrong for being
my one and only lifelong friend
I can sit with myself and feel
love and happiness
I don't judge myself
I'm the last person I talk to every night
So my words better carry kindness and care
Words of encouragement
to get through the night
I'm the first person
I see in the morning
I give myself
what I need

An Intense Act

Writing is an intense act
My eyes watch my hand
move across the page
leaving a path of words
that lead to beautiful notions
I felt it this morning
My head slowly spinning,
Dizzy with the power
of intentions poured out
Scribbled lines of love
I closed my eyes to reset
        contemplate the moment
My eyes and hands urgently working
to keep up with the inertia
of pen and paper in action

Mermaids

My assumptions about you have changed
Dear sweet one, you are like me
Swimming among the sharks
Who thirst for our creative blood
The tides of doubt under our feet
sweeps us deeper as we struggle
to steady our breath
We are in the same ocean
Swallowed by waves of fear and anger
We have come to the surface
Inhaling love of self
into our divine feminine being
Fully cherished by our own concept of who we are
Breaking through the ripple of thoughts
Not of our own minds but
what others perceive about us
We belong to our own realities
Yet we swim together like sisters
Mermaids birthed by Atargatis
Connected forever
in a way that is unspeakable
We serenade our souls
We have made the most profound assumption
Of ourselves
We are
        beautiful, feminine, powerful

These Hands

These two hands
        One to hold the pen
        One to hold the paper
bring creativity to life
The right, numb at times
from expressing myself
The left, weaker but still
important to the task

        These two hands
Cradle a baby's head
Hold an innocent hand
Clap for joy
Cover a worried face
Caress an achy body

        These two hands
Dry and cracked from dish water
Messy with daily life
Welcome new friends
Communicate with my soul

Thank God for
These two hands

Sweet Bread

As I lay in my grandmother's bed,
I hear creaks in the floor
that sound like wood ready to split apart
under brown worn linoleum
telling me my grandfather is getting breakfast.
The doorknob, worn by the touch of many
loving hands, twists, and rattles
footsteps down the hallway stairs
and across the wooden plank porch

A Saturday morning ritual that is burned into my senses.
The mission, to bring my brothers and me a sweet treat
My grandmother skillfully filled coffee grounds
and *canela* sticks into the percolator.
I remember the excitement of watching the hot steam
rise and dance inside the clear top handle

I anxiously await my pumpkin filled empanada
A piece of Mexican heaven
My morning treat
Pan dulce

Her Room

That tiny spare room was my little girl hideaway
no door, just a magical curtain
to a secret lair
My fingers traced over the indentions
that once held a hinge
I wondered who removed the door
and why?
Many nights I sat at the edge of the bed
Waiting for my grandmother
to come in and read to me
My eyes and mind scanned the dresser
> Perfume sprays
> Nail polish bottles
> A mirrored tray
> A scarf over the lamp shade
> created a warm glow

When would I have my own collection
of feminine indulgences?

Her room
Her things
> I dare not touch
> or peek inside boxes
It was perfect, she was perfect

How will my first granddaughter remember me?

Three Things About Me

I am Spiritual
        Angels guide me throughout the day
        never leaving my side
        I belong to a collective of beings
        who pass in and out of my reality
        What I release into the world
        comes back to me

I am Intuitive
        My inner being guides how I move through life
        I allow my body
        and inner dialogue to dictate my decisions
        well-being is the goal

I am Creative
        There is a well deep within
        full of ideas and passion
        spilling over, ready to be free
        Life flows from my pen
        yearning to fill time and space
        with like minded individuals

What are three things about you?

A Cosmic Blend

I have learned
important things
are not readily seen

I could list titles and labels
put on me since birth,
but these are not
Who I am

Many essentials
stir together
in a cosmic blend
which shapes my essence

The most important substances*
Spirituality
Self-Awareness
Creativity

*In no particular order

In My Power

I might be fifty plus
Years have come and gone
My eyes need help to see
My ears don't easily pick up voices
My skin, a little dry
My hair, a little gray
I get tired more easily
I'm passed my childbearing years

But I can create a world
where I am in control
You might not see
with your eyes, but you will
feel my presence
smell my sweet energy
hear my dynamic stride

If you thought I was near the end
I'll tell you-
Don't count me out yet
I'm just getting started
I'm in my power

Beyond Repair

This vase was whole and perfect
before it was handled without care
The hands that held it
Smudged its glossy finish

Those hands lost their grip
not knowing its weight
Smashed to the ground
broken beyond repair
You can't fill in the lines
with glue and lies

This vase still holds water
that gently weeps from the fractures
Close your eyes and feel with your hands
the slight imperfections
that catch across your fingertips

It's now a treasure to itself
They way it should have been
Love only a true heart gives
Careful, gentle hands
Give back its value

Broken Dreams

Broken down dreams can be rebuilt
But what does it take to begin the repair?

Clear away the debris that has landed
        around years of disappointments
Sweep shards of promises slowly fallen
        leaving dust on once shiny optimism

It will take time
like all projects
worth restoring

It's Never Too Late

My age only tells me
How many times
I have been around the sun
How does that determine where
I should be in my life?

The earth's movement does not decide
when inspiration comes to me
A paper calendar can't note
the successes of my passion

I have a purpose and it does not
revolve around a ticking clock.
I am the timekeeper in my world.

TV Land

I am Sam
      Samantha that is
Bewitched by self concept
I can wiggle my nose
Get whatever I want
Nothing can stop my magic

I am Genie
      Out of my bottle
A nod of my head sets me free
Arms crossed to show
Who's the one in charge

I am a Wonder Woman
      Superhero to myself
Wavy brown hair
Perfect white skin
My magic tied up
In imagination

These characters spoke to me
The powerful TV land women
with men under their feet

They love with spells
Change the world with a blink
I feel their wisdom and humor

No longer make believe
Because I believe in me

Magic is Real

A little girl with magical ideas
never forgets her once imagined power
The butterflies swatted away
by time and second guesses

The hope of a secret world
       hiding beneath the overgrown grass
       chopped by the steel blades
       of society's views of girlhood

A spark here and there
cause her to wonder
if the power is real inside of her
But opinions ensure she
       puts away the glittering thoughts
       that once filled her mind
A woman now aching for magic

There's no room for doubt
She remembered her gifts
       the essence of power

Breath of Wonder

I close my eyes and inhale

A breath of wonder
flows over my face
          and through my hair

My thoughts steaming through the windy night
The cool air refreshing my soul

          Imaginings of my thoughts
being carried away
Reaching a journey's end

I exhale and see- at last

From a Dream

         Imprinted on my heart
              burned into my soul
I carry your memory always
within

         Time and distance do not heal
             longing to see you
You are a piece of my being
 as I awaken

         I still feel your presence
             I hope you feel my love
radiating like warm waves
of the sun

Royal Blue Morning

I love the blueness of the morning just before sunrise
Am I the only one to stop and stare at its majestic entry?
The navy sky, an ocean of wonder
         A blur between reality and what might be
When I stare out
                  chin in my palm
I feel all things are possible

The transition is almost complete
I treasure this short time
I sit and wonder
         feeling peace in my day
I love this time of day,
 my royal blue morning

Artist of Wonder

Daydreaming
an accepted part of who I am
essential to my well being
not a childish activity

Daydreaming
a time of deep contemplation
a time of escape
a space of comfort and creativity

Daydreaming
A way to understand myself
A way to love myself
a fantastical fairytale life

A Daydreamer?
　　　An artist of wonder

A Love Letter

I will write myself
A love letter
       with a lipstick kiss
       Sprayed with pink petal Baby Soft scents
       Blended with woodsy pulp
       Sprinkled with affirmations that hug my heart

I am the writer, the poet
I impress upon myself

How amazingly my words
comfort the parts that need
a gentle message

Tilt

I thought I had let it all go
The fear that held me back for so long
still exists inside of me.

Sometimes it seems
trapped by walls
Bumping and sliding
inside of a pinball machine
Yet, I control the levers
I keep fear bouncing around
Hitting obstacles
with no point value

Why do I continue to play
within my mind
and keep it going?

It's time to end it
My hands slowly drop
letting my thoughts slip pass
the lever to lose the game
I should have stopped entertaining it
years ago

Gimme Shelter

Was it ok to shelter me, protect me from the pain?
No, I needed to feel and breathe
I needed to dig myself out of the rubble
of hopes and dreams that crumbled
and left a mess of emotions around my feet

Would it be so bad to experience
a world that is not perfect?
I needed to learn imperfect ways
as to triumph with strength

Rips and tears can be repaired
I would come back changed but strong
That shelter created to keep me
hidden from guilty pleasures
was a house of cards
ready to fall at the slightest breath

Artist Date

      I gave myself flowers
sipped on Chai tea latte
savored a walnut, carrot muffin
nibbled on fresh fruit

      It all sounds so simple
Yet, I showed my inner artist
She is loved and appreciated
I showed myself how to love me

Someone's Dreams

The little girl had given up
Her dreams were too distant
The life she longed for
no longer possible

But a woman emerged and remembered
the little girl's dreams
Through fear, doubts, and tears
she reached out a trembling hand
And pulled her back into the land of make-believe

Maybe those visions have changed
but the essence of being heard
resides in a new light

It's never too late
to save your own dream

And that little girl pulled the woman
Through the looking glass
on a ship shaped of clouds
passing a full moon

The little girl brought the woman
back to where dreams still exist

When I'm At Ease

I am most at ease with people
who can accept my need for silent moments
Sometimes words alter the peacefulness
I scripted earlier in the day

I am most at ease when I can have
a meaningful conversation over small talk
I'd rather know and share feelings
through rough storms than chit-chat
about rain and wind

I am most at ease with people
who graciously accept a keepsake
rather than shower me with gifts
but I promise I will appreciate it.

I am most at ease with people
who tell their story and don't mind
that I am just listening
Believe me, listening takes energy too
Eventually, I'll have a tale to share

April 22, 2022

How significant were this girl's actions?
The growing need to write down the events of a long
school day.
Finally receiving a little book she knew would change
something.
How profound that Holly Hobbie diary would be.
 Important memories kept safe by a flimsy lock.
Unrecognizable secrets and intense emotions of a 5th
grade heart.
A ten-year-old making sure her well-being was not
wrapped around reminders of school girl exaggerations of
love, found and lost.
Pages torn from the book of a young girl's mind.

If only adolescence had not come in to ridicule this prac-
tice.
If only the ritual emptying out had not been clouded
or blocked from the joy of a young heart.

She'd be stronger, more aware, ready to deal with the
challenges that changed her
into a self-conscious, people pleasing person.
She knew what would happen and tried to help, but it was
too late.
She was inside of a young adult drowning in a pool of
awkwardness and inadequacies.

It would take decades to find where her magic lies
Now a woman, she found her way back to acceptance

She picked up a journal and a pen once again.

Delightful

Does Tiffany make a candy necklace?
The treasure of young girl
 with the luxury for a grown ass woman!

Has Chanel made a sweet spritz?
A fragrance of youthful memories
captured in a bouquet of flowers and fruits!

What Secret is Victoria hiding?
A lingerie set to swaddle the insecurities
 of a teenager's unmentionable thoughts!

Charm of youth
Delight for a woman

Save Me

If I could go back, I would save you
You would only have to tell me
in your little, soft voice
who or what made you sad

It's strange to think of you as in the past
waiting for me to grow up and love you
You are not alone anymore
You are snuggled deep inside the safe chambers of my heart

I've learned how to protect you, but I still want to go back
Save you from loneliness

Two Windows

I remember your neon lights
green against a black sky
gave me peace from where I was

When I looked out of the left window
I could see rooftops and a skyline
that hold my childhood in mind

The right window faced out
to a section of the neighborhood
a mystery, train tracks and trees
I had walked those streets before
looking down on it was a curiosity

I still dream about that little section
of my childhood
The city block I visited often
I see it so clearly in my dreams
I prefer to go there in memory
I wish I had lived there as a kid
It remains alive and vibrant in visions
When I need a place to call home

Memories

Sometimes I hate thinking about memories
My eyes barely able to hold back the tears
that burn my cheeks and blur my vision

My throat tightens around a lump
It hurts to swallow
        It hurts my heart too

And these are the happy ones
that break me into pieces
During moments of sudden reminiscing

A Kind of Day

Today is the kind of day
when I need creativity
I need a poem
I need a story
I need magic

My nervous system
is sensing all of those
old ways that once
played on and on

My heart palpitating
My breathing shallow
A jittery bundle of nerves

I need imagination
I need music
I need my pen and paper

It's out of control
for a little while
But a creative burst
will calm and soothe
this kind of day

A little Secret

I had a little secret (wink)
I told my mother what I did
She had a disapproving comment
I guess she's who instilled the idea
That I should stay covered up
But I see my body as sacred

I didn't feel any different
I'm sure no one cared
Except for my mother
Who wasn't even there

I didn't feel ashamed
I still felt like myself
except that I had some knowledge
that other shoppers didn't have
I wanted to know how it would feel
to be in public
without wearing a bra (sigh of relief)
to Walmart this morning

Life went on
        as I figured

Three Places

Chicago -
- My childhood town
- Memories stretch where my eyes no longer see
- Commercial Ave
- Immaculate Conception School
- Twenty-seven years of my life spent here
- Still a place of mystery
- Some neighborhoods never explored

Hammond -
- Just thirty minutes away from home
- Indiana is new for me
- This is where I learned about
- Vacation Bible School, Strack's grocery store, and recycling
- My children's hometown now

Schererville -
- Grass cut and treated regularly
- Kids playing without a care
- Deer crossing and owls hooting
- Hawks swooping
- Lonely swan in the pond

Where to next?

Free Time

I see your face
I know your life
Anxiously awaiting free time

to feel sand on your toes
sharing time with loved ones
digging holes with your feet
shoveling sand in a bucket
swimming in the cold waves
splashing with your arms
sunning your sweet skin

You held your mami's hand
as you left for the day
Your tired body ready for a nap

Summer will miss you

Beach Day

The tent took forever to pitch
Sand was blowing everywhere
Teens stormed the sand
Games of catch put me on guard
People ignore dogs and grilling rules

No peace to read my book
No peace to write my dreams

Listen

Intuition is real
in the pit of my stomach
to the point of queasiness
That's my sign
She has kept me alert

My heart picks up on nuances
I can feel energy
contrasting with mine

I have ignored her at times
Talked myself out of the warnings

I have learned to listen
She has refused to stay silent

Don't Think Small

I don't have time to think small
I only have my right hand to create
The words strung together
like the beads on a friendship bracelet

My hand goes numb
when the motions repeat too long
So much time spent creating lesson plans
never enough time to plan my dreams
My eyes burn and blur reading other people's stories,
self-help, and poetry for too long

I've just discovered the greatness
with my inner artist trapped
in a fifty-two year old body
Although my spirit feels young
The physical body grows old
I don't have time to think small

The Neglected Idea

She came to me one November
I remember how insistent
all around and through my head
until I was able to click away at the keyboard
I dreamt of her
I breathed her
I envisioned her
She would be the center of my daydreams
but I wasn't strong enough to hold her
I wondered what others would think of her character
Did she speak correctly?
Was she interesting enough to catch the world's attention?
"No" I thought
Stop while you haven't wasted any more time
Go on with your life

She left
Why would she stay?
I refused to give her life
and she wilted like a dead flower
in a glass vase,
Neglected

Inspiration

Talk to me, baby
I've waited so long
just to see
what you look like
I want to hear your voice
I imagine your sound
like angels in a choir
so loud and beautiful
my head would turn in a snap
I've heard you come to people unexpectedly
and tell them something that changes their lives
I don't do small talk
You need to stick around
fill my ears with your sweet voice
I promise not to ignore you
We'll engage any time of the day
You've had my attention before
I was the foolish one
Who thought you'd stay
I'm older and wiser
Just talk to me
I'll listen forever

Self-Giving

I will remain a writer
My ultimate act
of self love and care

I am a writer
I am the greatest
from my own point of view

That is my gift to myself
to write my heart out
 An audience does not make it valuable

The satisfaction and pleasure
when creating from within
Is my treasure

Seeing Myself

I saw myself for the first time
When I broke free from myself
I looked towards my feet
  Fear
    Insecurity
      Foolishness
were gently falling
like feathers from a bird's wings
Stretched out and flowing
Ready to soar

I Looked windward and saw
for the first time
my own scared feelings
Now afraid of my own eyes
I exposed these thoughts
to the wonderful light
and they vaporized like mist

I was in control
Beliefs made into a pillar of salt
by my inward stare

Happy At Last

I wept and sighed at how
the creative goddess within
was happy at last
to be recognized and celebrated

She waited many years
to be liberated
to show her glorious power

Draped in pure white silk
A halo of delicate flowers
Holding my words in her hands

Strength

It's funny how
I've had this strength
inside of me since birth,
Yet as an adult it came out
when I found the little girl
Once again

A Simple Message

There's something on my mind
but I don't have the words yet

Stirrings in my heart tell me
to write a simple message

I don't know who will read it
but it needs to be set free

When the words find me,
I will give them life
And, hopefully, a place in time

Dear Friend

My poor dear friend
I have ignored you for much too long

I think we met when we were eight
We spent lots of time together
But I didn't think you were enough

In my teens,
I couldn't have anything to do with you

In my twenties,
I found you again, but there was tension
It was a struggle to keep you around
So, we once again parted ways

I thought about you a lot over the next two decades
I wondered where you were
I tried to make contact several times

Now, you are back
I appreciate your presence
I value our bond
Our relationship is solid
Our hearts are one
Forever, my dear friend

Memories Still Bloom

What should I do with these dried up roses?
Should I press them in a book with your photograph?
I'll forget the petals are there
        stuck between blank pages
The memories continue to bloom
When I close my eyes to see you once more

Days Like This

It's days like this
      I need to step outside
      I look to the sky to calm myself,
            the clouds to find answers

When a deep breath isn't enough,
I allow the wind to move through me

It cools my skin
It relaxes my neck
It plays with my hair

Only the wind settles my fears
On days like this

Elements

The sun,
        the moon,
                and me
A cosmic threesome
I'm surrounded by voluptuous bodies
that belong to the Universe

Clouds,
        wind,
                and energy
Flowing through the trees
I'm comforted by the elements
that cool my sultry flesh

Day,
        night,
                and dew
We are visible to all who pay attention
to the passionate morning
On my way to nowhere

When There Is Little Joy

What will it take for me to see
I am losing the battle
against everyday life?
When there is little joy,
getting out of bed is a job.
I'm tired even before I arrive
I'm beat before lunch
The clock ticks louder
Turning pages sounds like thunder

Am I wasting time?
Am I making a difference?
Am I just surviving?

I look around this place
Dirty carpets, windowless rooms
Soulless scholars, heartless heroes
Nothing is aligned with my heart
I force my attention towards
Time off and weekend breaks

An Unexpected Circumstance

I hope you find what you're looking for
A dream told you to leave your life behind
and look for answers in paradise

An unexpected circumstance
brought you here to say goodbye
A moment I'll play over in my head

You're taking a chance starting over
Or are you trying to turn back time?
Some words were never spoken
All you have are memories

Movement keeps you sane
Urgency keeps you on edge
Once that wears off,
I hope you found what you were looking for
and you have peace at last.

Sugar Cane

In the heart
of an asphalt jungle
a proud brown warrior
partakes in a morning ritual
awakened to venture out
through concrete pathways
surrounded by steel trunks
through flickers of sunlight.
He emerges with a gift
presented to his young children.
A stalk of sweet grass
carefully sliced into bite sized pieces
to enjoy and treasure
A sweet treat burned in my tongue's memory

I'm learning

I'm growing
I'm shifting

I'm moving through the dark
My eyes closed
Searching for my place in time

Tears blur and sting
the corners of my eyes
Blurry visions become clear

I'm thinking
I'm feeling
I'm creating

I'm slowly gliding through nothingness
My hands guide my spirit
I'm lost and found at the same time
in a place scary yet comforting

I'm losing myself in the moment
I'm between daydreams and reality

Finding My Way

My take away
      from years spent searching
      for validation
      Eyes tired and dry
      thoughts spinning

Never have I been
      more conscious
      more present
      more satisfied
         with the process

Of finding my way
      Through the trials of adolescence
      Correcting the errors of foolish judgements

I became aware
      I already had the magic within me

I Still Exist

What were you thinking?
What thoughts went through your head?
Did you erase me from your memory?
that *is* what you attempted
Were there flashbacks,
Still frame memories all at once
that made your head spin?
Are you better off now?

Did you think I wouldn't notice?
Will you wish you had waited
before you made that decision?
Did you read my name?
Did you see my face?
Do you blame me for your broken
promises and unfulfilled dreams?
What will you do without me now?

No matter how hard you try to erase me,
my thoughts are here to stay
I exist

Generations of Hands

I hold a photograph of a woman
Sitting in a chair
My eyes search the image
I am mesmerized
by her *hands*
Fingers gently tangled and knotted
My great-great grandmother
She was a skilled artisan
My great grandmother was a creator too
She had to be or she would starve
alongside her children
My grandmother would inherit
Her mother's *hands*, talents, and skills

Cooking
Sewing
knitting
crocheting
Surviving

Creativity flows through generations of *hands*, yet
My hands have never known those skills
lost to modern innovation
But *my hands* create with words
My pen- the needle, hook, or wooden spoon

Journaling
Writing
Composing
Searching

My hands
I imagine
Being gently cupped and guided
by all those other ancestral *hands* that transcend
time and space

Red Leaf

Red leaf blowing in the wind
Alone in the greenish, brown grass
You tumble and glide
Waiting to be lifted
Taken to new heights

You no longer belong
to the branch that nurtured you

Will you end up in a river
Swirling with ripples,
raked over in a pile
burned like sage
Or
Free?

Dancing My Dream

Dancing to clear space
Making room in my body
for my dream feels good
      a living entity
      inside of me
She is real

Moving with me
and all through me
my dream needs to stretch
      and feel safe
      I give it life
She needs to breathe

We feel peace and rhythm
No longer stiff and unbalanced
Movements memorized
      comfortable steps
      energy flowing
We dance to be free

How I Feel

I feel my arm
I know it exists
It feels seen

My bones are strong
My skin and muscles relaxed
My elbow sharp and bent

It's a little sensitive
to my own touch
Squeezing and touching

The arm I consider the weaker
Of the two has shown me
That I am strong

A Splendid Thought

My body no longer creates living souls,
but my spiritual being gives birth to new ideas

My inner artist is young and fertile
She gives life and light to my realty and my world

My world is sacred and sanctified through new life
every day my mind and thoughts shape who I am

I am a creative being
What a splendid thought

Escape

There are beliefs that still keep me
in a state I continually
try to escape

I wrote them down to see
what I needed to change

A paper safety net
to capture and release
the heaviest thoughts
in my imagined prison

Dec 1, 2022

My blood still spills
Even through numb skin
       I thought this would never happen to me again
       I was passed not feeling
       I moved on from heartache
       I was strong again
       I had a grip on life
       I was powerful
       I could never be numb again
       I still need help to get through
the struggles
that my blood has shown me

New Year

Time ticks away
leaving a trail
of hopes, dreams, yearnings
loss, let downs, heartache
Marks to look back on

Time moves forward
entering a path
of new desires
eager beginnings
Steps to look ahead

We play the games
   Grapes in our mouths
   Money clenched in our fists
   Suitcases rolling at our feet
Anything to help ease into
Space and time
Yet explored

And we begin again

Dread and Resistance

Why do I continue
To do things that
Never bring me joy?

Is it just a bad habit
Or do I get some pleasure
from the pain?

The thought of doing things
that I don't want to do
Creates dread and resistance

My senses dull
My body aches
and stiffens

What is the price I pay?
Peacefulness torn in half
Tears pushed back from my eyes
Sown through my throat

I have to leave and watch
my body go through the motions
I'm at a safe distance
and repeat one more time

Is It A Dream?

I close my eyes
I feel the sun on my face
The air is soft and sweet
Smooth velvet petals
on my fingers
Is it a dream?
Is it imagination?
What is real?
Petals fall to the ground
Time slips through my hands
as a tear melts into my skin
my feet barely able to keep balance
I'm floating away
The wind carrying me
to my safe place
where a field
surrounded by hills
gives me enough time
to inhale
and exhale joy

Alone-

> Only the sounds of myself
> Breathing a steady rhythm
> Heartbeats tapping at my chest
> Buzzing in my ears
> My hands gently creating
> Honey on my lips
> The only time my mind resets
> A gift with no price tag
> No better way to spend time

>> -alone

Bird

Was I meant to be a bird
flying freely in the sky
floating on the wind
through a soft, cool cloud?

Have I been clipped?
my wings shredded
the sky seems familiar
yet I am closer to the ground
I struggle to spread myself
across time and memory

Was I meant to fly alone
or part of a flock
that surrounds me most days?
The weight of my humanity
is too much to bare on a branch
designed for rest and discovery

Could I be so free?
the world a sky of graceful flight
maybe someday I will float
as mystically as a feather
falls beautifully to earth

Will I sing as lively as the flute
which summons freedom to the level of my mind's voice?
I think
        I was meant to be a bird

Wind

The wind flows through my body
Its sounds are waves of wonder
It carries me across time
and dimensions unknown
The wind loves my hair
It gently tugs away negative feelings
that attach to its roots
The wind caresses my face
It cools the warmth of worry
leaving a pink mark of its invisible hands
The wind is my comfort
He never leaves me unnoticed
His arms hold me tight
when he comes to me at night
The wind clothes me
with waves of tangled streams
only visible to my eyes

Treasure

A treasure buried deep within my being
Awaits to be discovered, not by thieves
but those who appreciate gems
Nuggets of wisdom locked away
to preserve its value
A string of pearls to wear
for the world to admire
Luxury timepieces outlast earthly possessions
They search for jewels to pawn
but this treasure cannot be bought
Brilliance that turns tears
into diamonds rolling off my cheek
They will see its glory
but not with eyes

Treasure seen by the soul
Treasure felt with the heart
The true language of creativity

I Was You

You came in a dream
to remind me of who I use to be
Happiness on your face
I watched you from afar
Smooth white skin
Soft brown hair
You were living my dream
The true story of my life
I knew who you were
The minute I saw you
Surrounded by love and light

You were me
I am you
I still wait to see you
come back to me
and we'll live out our story
As one

A long, dark path

The path is dark and long
I hear my footsteps
crunch on fallen leaves
I can't see passed the trees
My vision weakened
by the pitch black sky
No stars
No moon
My heart thumps against my lungs
as the cool air swirls inside
How much farther must I walk
to reach a safe place?
I can wait for the sun,
but then I'll need to be still
I want to move around
Feel with my mind
Feel with my soul
Finally reach the other side
of this dark, long path

Pages From Within

Like leaves in the whispering wind
blank pages rustle my thoughts
Words flowing through
a subconscious blue inked stream
   Written expressions of time
   Tokens of remembrances
   Sentiments of my life
   Tangled Remnants of memories
   Givings from my soul
   Mosaic flashbacks

An artist's gift,
   one heart to yours,

My pages
   from within

About Author

Laura Serratos is a Mexican-American, English Language Arts teacher, writer, author, certified life coach, and poet in Northwest Indiana. Laura earned a B.A. in English and an M.Ed. in School Administration from Purdue University Calumet. She has spent twelve years in education where she has been touched tremendously by the lives and stories of her students who come from all walks of life.

At a very young age, Laura knew that one day she would see her name in the title of her own book. Many weekends were spent at her grandparent's home in the South Chicago neighborhood where her imagination took off. Armed with paper, markers, and a stapler, the seed of authorship was planted in the heart of a young eight-year-old girl. Laura dreamed of one day telling her story of love, laughter, and the sometimes-hard realities of life. A bit of this dream has been fulfilled with her debut poetry collection I, Too Bloom. Since the release of her poetry book, Laura has continued working on her dream of becoming a fulltime professional writer.

Laura Serratos lives in Schererville, Indiana where she enjoys spending many special occasions with her family at her home. When she is not teaching and writing, you could find her engrossed in poetry, fiction, or self-help. More important hobbies include traveling to discover food and culture, wishing upon a star, and listening to music that inspires her imagination.

Laura Serratos

www.ingramcontent.com/pod-product-compliance
Lightning Source LLC
Chambersburg PA
CBHW051318120626
46547CB00015B/2293